Investing for Beginners:

A Practical Guide to Financial Freedom and Successful Stock Market Investing

Steve Morgan

Copyright © 2016 Steve Morgan

All rights reserved.

ISBN: 1537597884
ISBN-13: 978-1537597881

DEDICATION

This book is dedicated to my beautiful wife and children. You drive and inspire me to be a better man each and every day.

CONTENTS

Introduction	1
Chapter 1: Why Should You Start Saving Young?	3
Chapter 2: Stock Market Fundamentals to Know	9
Chapter 3: How to buy Stocks	21
Chapter 4: Bulls, Bears, and Pigs	24
Chapter 5: Asset Allocation and Diversification Introduction	27
Chapter 6: Popular Investment Classes	35
Chapter 7: Managing Your Investment Portfolio	39
Conclusion	49

INTRODUCTION

I want to thank you and congratulate you for downloading the book, *"Investing for Beginners: A Practical Guide to Financial Freedom and Successful Stock Market Investing"*.

Why is it so Important to Start Saving Money at a Young Age?

Some young people have a hard time understanding why they should make an effort to start saving money. Since it's the norm to lavishly spend money on fun pursuits, when you can afford it, not many people think of an alternative to this. But instead of using all of the extra income you have, you should begin saving it as young as possible, in order to make sure that you have a safe and stable future. Life is very unpredictable, and it's impossible to know what will happen. One day, you could be working at a great place and have no visible reason to think this will end, and then, unexpectedly get laid off and find yourself having a hard time making ends meet.

Why Learning Investment is a Wise Pursuit:

When you make it a point to save money, you will be protecting yourself against life's unforeseen difficulties. And when you invest, if you choose to do so, you will have a chance to earn much more than you would have expected to, growing your money exponentially. This book will explore all of the reasons why saving money young is the best course of action, as well as investment basics to get you started in the world of stocks.

Would it be great if you could own a business, without needing to go to work? Envision a life where you could see your business grow before your very eyes, collect money, and possibly even retire early. To some of you, this may sound like an impossible dream, but this ideal is more possible than you may believe. In this book, we will show you real, actionable methods for making this dream a reality. Thanks again for downloading this book, I hope you enjoy it!

CHAPTER 1: WHY SHOULD YOU START SAVING YOUNG?

We've all heard the age old wisdom that saving early is a wise idea. This is likely not the first time that you have heard this recommendation, and there's a good reason for that. For anyone who could use a safety net, some extra money, or the chance to retire early, following this simple advice is a must. Compound interest (which we will discuss in further detail a bit later) is reason enough, but there are multiple other reasons that this habit will help you immensely in life. Here are some more reasons why you should look into this option.

Reasons to Start Saving Young:

- **You will be Wasting Less:** Sure, earning money is very helpful for countless reasons, but decreasing your spending habits is the quickest and simplest way to grow your savings account. As soon as you commit to saving, you will become aware of all of the unnecessary cash you're wasting on nonessential areas. Fortunately, nearly every person out there will discover that making a budget helps you realize what you can sacrifice without lowering your standard of living. All it takes is a willingness to see, plan, and follow through.

- **A Higher Chance of Compatible Friendships:** The earlier you change your spending and saving habits, the more likely you are to find people to involve in your social group that share the same principles. Not only will this help you to have fun with life without spending an arm and a leg, but you will learn to look for social activities to partake in that don't cost a lot.

    As soon as you are ready to find your lifelong partner, you will have already created the financial habits that will be with you for life. This will heighten your chances of finding someone to retire with who shares your principles and can help you stay on track.

- **Better Chances of Finding Great Opportunities:** Hardly anyone knows for sure what their career path will look like when they graduate. There's also the fact that many people change their mind about their major somewhere in the course of their studies, which, unfortunately, comes with income gaps or even wage cuts. When you commit to saving money early on in life, your safety net will let you take advantage of chances you may have missed out on if you had never done so, such as investing, taking extra time off, or exploring your hobby a bit more thoroughly.

- **You will also be Growing your Confidence:** Increasing your savings account is a great way to increase your level of confidence, since you will have an awareness that you possess assets to get you through any hard times that may come. When you start saving money early on, you can rest easy with the knowledge that your family is safe from financial hardships in the future. This will allow you to take bolder steps in your career, and life in general. The fear you may have had about losing your career or getting laid off will be lessened or even non-existent, allowing you to take chances and succeed in ways that would have been impossible before.

- **Your Life will get Better:** It's far too common, unfortunately, that people live with stress due to their finances being limited. This can cause a lot of strain, and even unhealthy behaviors such as over-eating or addictions, causing exhaustion and further fueling the cycle of stress. This stress will eventually cause conflicts with the family or friends due to emotions constantly being on overdrive.

    The art of living frugally and developing a habit of saving will allow you to prevent this dangerous pattern. You won't be stressed as much because you will have lowered your unnecessary spending, making your lifestyle easier and cheaper to sustain. There is no substitute for feeling fulfilled in life, especially when that involves a harmonious household with healthy relationships.

This should give you an idea of how important this habit is to start as early as you can. There is no reason you should be investing excuses or reasons not to start building your savings now, while you have a chance. Even starting with five dollars a week is better than nothing. Commit to taking that first step, and allow your habits to grow along with your account. Now that we've discussed the importance of this path, we can get down to the specifics of how to do it successfully.

Tips for Getting Started on your Savings Journey:

- **Before Spending Money, Save First:** Whenever you find yourself with some extra money, you must make a habit of removing the portion that will go into your savings, before you start spending it. What is incredible and effective about this method is that as soon as you've taken out what will go into your savings pot, you will know that you have some extra money to spend as you wish to.

    The money that you remove should never be viewed as spending money, but it is important to make sure you're enjoying what you make and not only saving it. This way, the process feels more like a worthy choice, rather than a strict obligation that you grow to resent.

- **Ask your Parents to get Involved:** This step depends entirely on your family's financial situation, as well as your relationship with your folks, but it's worth looking into. Ask your parents to see if they are willing to match the money you put away, to help you with developing your smart habits of saving. A lot of parents would be thrilled that their child is making the smart choice to begin a savings account, and be happy to help establish their good habits, early on.

- **Think about Opportunity Costs of What you Spend Money on:** This is a financial term that applies to various aspects of life. You can see this term as the losing of possible gains from other choices when one choice is specified. For example, you could either purchase a bicycle for $100, or put your money into your safety net account. Say that that account has an interest rate of 12 percent that gets compounded each year. The $100 you decided to invest will grow to become $310 within a decade.

  Due to the fact that you cannot touch this money for a decade, that might not sound significant, so think of it on a bigger scale. Imagine adding $100 to your account every year, and what that would end up becoming. That is quite a significant amount of money, all because you decided to invest an amount that you didn't need to spend in the first place. Imagine how much more you could save within an extra decade. This is why starting earlier (at age 30, rather than 40, for example) is the best choice.

- **Start a Coin Jar:** Though this may sound insignificant, it really adds up after a while. Start throwing your extra change into a jar in your house and watch how it builds up.

- **Don't Carry Cash:** This simple tip is probably the most effective of all for saving money. If you don't have cash in your pocket, you won't even view spending as an option. You will also protect yourself against buying items on impulse while out and about. Make it a point to become disciplined about what you spend money on, narrowing it down to absolute necessities such as bills, shelter, clothing, and food.

- **Decide on an Amount to Save with Each Paycheck:** Once you've opened up an account for saving that has a great interest rate, it's time to decide how much of your check you will put into it each time you get paid. This will ensure that you stick to your plan and that your money is growing while it sits in the account. Plus, it will make it so that you have to take extra steps to spend that money, making this less likely.

- **Increase your Odds of Retiring Early:** If you start to save just 10 years earlier in life, this can end up adding up to thousands and thousands of extra capital over a person who started saving later on.

The key here is to start as soon as you can. Doing this as young as possible will make your capital multiple much quicker, and you will be ingraining lifelong habits that will benefit you for year to come. This is a simple choice that many grown people fail to follow through on. Once you're into the habit of self-discipline early on, you can handle loans and credit cards in a cautious way, avoiding the pitfalls of debt that imprison so many people.

Know the Benefits of Compound Interest:

This type of interest is calculated using both the starting principal and on the interest accumulated over periods from the past of a loan or deposit, as well. Compound interest is helpful to think of as the interest that gets applied to existing interest, and makes loans or deposits multiply quicker than simple, basic interest, which relies only on the principal, basic amount. How much the rate of your compound interest will gather and accumulate depends upon how often the compounding takes place. The more you compound, the higher your interest rate will go.

CHAPTER 2: STOCK MARKET FUNDAMENTALS TO KNOW

Stocks are a wonderful category of tools in finance that are considered one of the best ways to grow your money. Stocks are a portion, and often the foundation, of any quality portfolio of investments. Once you begin your journey to economic freedom, you must have a decent awareness and understanding of the way stocks function, and the ways they get traded on the market. During recent decades, more and more people are becoming interested in learning about the stock market. This was, at one time, an avenue only reserved for the rich, and has now transformed into an option for average people to grow their wealth.

Trading- An Increasingly Popular Road to Growing your Capital:

These considerations, in addition to technological advances in trading, have made the markets more open than ever. As a result, just about anyone can get into owning and trading stocks. Although they are popular, though (who doesn't want to grow their income?), stocks are not fully understood by most people. People get their information from other enthusiasts who, though well-intentioned, unfortunately are also not accurately informed about the workings of the market. The odds are, if you have any passing interest in investing, you have already heard about fantastic sources for "hot tips", or even warnings which don't make sense.

Beware of Misinformation about Stocks and Trading:

A lot of the wrong information out there has come about from the mentality of trying to get rich quickly and easily. People believed that trading stocks was the key to earning lots of money instantly without having to risk anything. Although stocks do lead to large amounts of money, they do not exist without inherent risks. The only way to protect yourself, as much as possible, against these risks, is to become educated about the process. The best way to protect your assets in the market is to know precisely where it is you are placing your hard-earned bucks.

Due to these inescapable facts, you should find quality information whenever possible, and this book is a great place to start. This book will give you what you need to start making your own, informed investing choices. So, let's start with the basics.

What, Exactly, is a Stock?

To put it as simply as possible, it is a share of ownership of a business. A stock stands for your claim to the earnings and assets of a company. As soon as you gain more stocks, the stake that you hold in that company grows along with that. The words "equity" and "shares" are synonymous for stocks and can be used interchangeably.

What does it Mean to be the Owner of Stock?

When you hold stock in a company, this means you're a shareholder, and one of the multiple owners of that specific business. This means that you have a (usually small) claim to whatever that business owns. Technically, it means that you are in possession of a tiny amount of everything related to that company. Since you are an owner, this makes you entitled to a portion of the earnings of that company, along with the rights to vote for matters related to that stock.

What is a Stock Certificate?

When you purchase a stock, it will be represented by something known as a stock certificate. This signifies the proof that you own a portion of that company, and comes in the form of a sheet of paper. Since our world grows increasingly modernized, chances are, you won't ever glimpse your certificate, due to brokerages holding onto records digitally. This can also be called the "in street name" way of holding onto shares. The reason for this is that it makes shares simpler to work with and trade. Previously, when someone wished to sell off their shares, they had to take the physical sheets of paper to a physical brokerage. But nowadays, a simple phone call or click online will get you trading, making the process simpler.

What being a Shareholder does *not* Signify:

When you are one of the shareholders of a company, you do not get to decide what occurs in the daily goings on of that company. Rather, a single vote for each share for electing the director's board at yearly meetings is about all you actually have a say in. For example, if you are a shareholder with Microsoft, it does not mean you have the right to call up the company's boss and let them know what you think the company should do or how things should be run. The way a company is managed should raise the value of that company for those holding shares.

It's a rare occurrence, but shareholders, at least theoretically, are able to vote to remove the current management of a company. The way it actually happens, however, rarely grants the average investor the ability to do so, since they often don't own a high enough number of shares to have that kind of say. It's typically rich entrepreneurs and investors of the institutional variety that have all the say. For the typical, average share holder, having no say in the management of the business isn't a problem; isn't the main appeal of this path being able to work *less*? The important part is that you have a right to a percentage of the profits from the company, some of which will be paid to you with dividends.

Equity versus Debt:

What motivation do businesses have for issuing stock? What is the benefit of sharing profits with so many people, rather than keeping the earnings themselves? Companies have to raise money to be successful, which is why they opt for this choice. This means that they can either borrow the capital in some way, or earn it by selling off portions of their business, or by stock issuing. Businesses are able to borrow money by receiving loans from financial centers or through bond issuing. Each of these methods for raising capital can be considered "debt financing", while stock issuing is known as equity financing.

Stock Issuing is Beneficial for Companies because:

- **The company doesn't have to pay that money back.**

- **There is no worry about payments for interest in the process.**

For their money, people who are holding shares receive a chance to earn money when the shares increase in value. When a private business issues their first stock sale, it's called an IPO (initial public offering).

Understanding the Differences with Financing using Equity vs. Debt:

This is an important distinction to be aware of, especially for beginners.

- **Debt Investment:** When you make a purchase of some type of debt investment (like a bond), you can be certain that your money (also called, in this situation, the principal) will be returned to you, in addition to payments of interest that were promised.

- **Equity Investment:** The above does not apply, however, when it comes to investments in equity. Once you decide to become an owner, you are taking on risk of that business becoming unsuccessful, at some point. Similar to how the owner of a smaller company cannot be certain that they will get a return, a shareholder also cannot be certain. When you are an owner, you have less of a claim to the assets than creditors.

If the business you have invested in liquidates and ends up going bankrupt, you will not receive any profit at all until the bondholders and banks have already been paid off. This is known as an important priority. It's true that a shareholder can make a decent amount when a business becomes successful, but it's possible that they could lose everything they invested if that business goes under or does not experience success.

How to View Risk with Investing in Stocks:

- **No Guarantees:** It's important to note that no guarantee can be made in terms of stocks on an individual level.

- **Not all Pay Dividends:** While it's true that some businesses will end up paying dividends, a lot of them will not. Firms are under no obligations to do this, even if they did at one time.

- **The Downside of not Receiving Dividends:** If they do not receive dividends, someone who invests will only have a chance to earn with the stock if it appreciates in the market. The negative aspect of this is that a stock can go bankrupt at any time, making your investment worthless.

Higher Risk = Better Chance of a Quality Return:

On the surface, risk may sound like a bad thing, but there is an upside to this. When you take on a higher risk, you are demanding a better return on what you have invested. For this reason, stocks are more popular than other avenues for investing, like savings accounts or bonds. Considering the long term of stocks, investing in them has shown average rates of return up to 12 percent. Two main types need to be known, when it comes to stocks. These are common and preferred.

Common Stocks:

When you hear someone referring to stocks, this is the type they are usually talking about. Common stocks are, obviously, common.

- **Covers Nearly all Stocks:** Actually, most stocks are issued using this format. The information that we covered in previous sections detailed some of the features of common stocks. They are shares that signify ownership of a small portion of a business, as well as a claim to a part of the earnings (the dividends) made by the company.

- **Higher Returns:** Better chances of earning money than other types of investments. This does, of course, come with some measure of risk. If the company is unsuccessful, you could lose your investment.

- **Variable Dividends:** This could be seen, by some, as a downside. Dividends are not guaranteed.

Preferred Stocks:

Many people think of preferred stocks are being more similar to debt than they are to equity. You can view them as between common shares and bonds. Here are some other defining characteristics of preferred stocks.

- **Ownership, but no Voting Rights:** Preferred stocks stand for a certain amount of ownership, but typically do not involve rights to voting. This varies from business to business.

- **Guaranteed Dividends:** Preferred shares mean that you, as an investor, will be guaranteed dividends at a fixed level, usually for an unlimited amount of time.

- **Preferred Stock holders get Paid First:** When it comes to common vs. preferred stocks, preferred holders get paid off after holders of debt, but before common stock holders.

- **Callable:** These types of stocks are often callable, which means that the business has a choice to buy stocks from shareholders (typically at a premium price), any time they wish.

The Differing Classes to Know about:

It's true that preferred and common stocks are the two main types. But, business can choose to customize differing types of stock however they choose. The main reason this happens is because businesses want the powers of voting to stay within a particular group. This means that differing types of shares are assigned differing rights for voting. One class, for example, could belong to a specific group who is assigned ten votes for each share, and another class could get issued to the larger number of traders who are assigned just one vote for each share. Classes of stock are usually assigned as either Class A or Class B.

Different Types of Exchanges:

The majority of stocks get traded using exchanges, or locations where sellers and buyers meet up to pick a price.

- **Physical Exchange Locations:** A number of exchanges are actual, real locations that involve trading floors where transactions are handled. We've all seen photos of trading floors, covered in traders signaling to each other, waving their arms, and yelling.

- **Virtual Exchange Locations:** This is a digital exchange location, involving a computer network where trades are conducted using the internet.

The entire point of the market for stocks is to make possible security exchanges between sellers and buyers, significantly lowering investment risks. Try to envision how hard it would get to sell off your shares the old-fashioned way, calling around to houses in the neighborhood in hopes of selecting the right buyer. It may help to think of the market as an advanced farmers' market that exists to hook up sellers and buyers.

The Secondary and Primary Markets:

Before proceeding, it's important to make a distinction between the secondary and primary markets. Keep in mind that trading stock from a business doesn't always involve that business directly.

- **The Primary Market:** This is the place where securities come from, using an IPO.

- **The Secondary Market:** Here, investors can trade securities that were issued previously, without worrying about the companies for issuing. When someone mentions the general stock market, they are referring to the secondary market.

The NYSE (or New York Stock Exchange):

If you have an interest in this topic, you have probably already heard of the best-known exchange on the planet, the NYSE. This exchange first started over two centuries ago, in the year 1792. America's largest corporations, such as Coca-Cola, McDonald's, and General Electric, opt for this market, also called the "Big Board".

Nasdaq- The Virtual OTC Market:

Nasdaq is the most popular of all digital exchanges, also known as an over-the-counter (or OTC) exchange market. Having no brokers on the floor or physical location, trading here is conducted using telecommunication, computers, and a group of dealers. There was a time when the biggest businesses out there were listed on NYSE alone, leaving stocks of a second tier to be traded on alternate exchange markets. However, the boom of technology near the dawning of the millennium shifted this paradigm. Today, several huge companies for technology find their home with Nasdaq, including Oracle, Intel, and Microsoft, leading Nasdaq to be a major competitor for the previously untouchable NYSE.

There are exchanges all around the planet, but markets in America are the biggest of all. Even so, they only represent a portion of complete investment in the world. London and Hong Kong are two main centers, as well. Prices for stocks shift each day due to forces in the market, meaning that prices of shares shift due to demand and supply. If there are more people out there wishing to purchase stocks (creating demand) than there are people who wish to sell stocks (supply), this causes the prices to increase. On the other hand, if there were more people who wanted to sell stocks than purchase them, the higher supply would cause the prices to go down.

How do People Decide Which Stocks to Favor and Avoid?

But understanding this interplay isn't the hard part. What some people find hard to understand is why investors choose certain stocks over others. This involves finding out the positives and negatives about particular companies. Countless answers exist for this particular issue, and nearly every investor has their unique strategies and ideas for determining that.

What Determines a Company's Value?

However, the main theory on this is that movements of the price of stocks show how investors perceive the value of that company. Many people make the mistake of equating the value of a company with the price of its stocks, but a company's value actually lies in market capitalization. Market capitalization is the price of a stock times the amount of outstanding shares of the company. To make this even more complicate, a stock's price is not just reflective of the current value of a company, but the expected growth to come in the future.

The Main Factor that Determines a Company's Value:

Perhaps the main factor determining a company's value is what that company ears, meaning the profits that businesses makes. No businesses can continue without profits, which makes perfect sense. If businesses never earn capital, they cannot continue as a business. Companies that are public must report what they earn quarterly (or four times annually).

These times (also known as earnings seasons) are paid attention to especially closely by Wall Street. This is because analysts decide on the potential future value of businesses based on the projection of their earnings. If the results of the quarterly information surprise investors (meaning that they are higher than people expect), prices will go up. If the results of the quarterly report show that the company did worse than people expected, they will see falling of prices.

What Else Changes Investors' Ideas of a Stock:

Earnings are not the only determination for influencing general attitudes toward stocks (which results in price changes). This entire process would be much simpler if that's all there were to it. For example, during the bubble of the dotcom era, a lot of online companies grew and had market capitalizations of high amounts, all without profiting whatsoever. As many people are aware, these high values didn't end up holding, leading to the majority of these online companies to shrink in value.

What influences the Movements of a Stock's Price?

Even so, prices not moving very much proves that factors outside of current profits are influencing stock prices. Professional investors have come up with countless indicators, ratios, and variables. While some of these are common and well known (like ratios of earnings and price), others are complex and more obscure. This may lead you to wonder what exactly causes stocks to change prices. The simplest way to explain this is that no one can say for certain.

CHAPTER 3: HOW TO BUY STOCKS

While some think that it's impossible to make predictions about the changes of stock prices, others believe that paying attention to movements of prices from the past, along with drawing up charts, will help you decide the best times to sell and purchase. One thing can be said for certain, and that is that volatility is always present in stocks, making them chance very quickly in terms of prices. Here are some basic principles to understand about the subject.

Important Points to Keep in Mind:

- **Demand and Supply:** Although it is much more complicated than this, demand and supply will play a large role in determining the prices of stocks in the market.

- **A Company's Value:** The stock price, multiplied by the amount of market capitalization, or outstanding shares, will show how valuable a business is. It doesn't work to try to compare prices of shares to determine this.

- **Expectations and Attitudes play a Large Role:** Although it's true that profits are what determine the way an investor will value companies, other indications exist that are used as tools to determine the prices of stocks. Ultimately, the expectations, attitudes, and sentiments are what affect the prices of stocks, making them all the more difficult to predict accurately.

- **No "one size fits all" Theory:** Although countless ideas exist out there for explaining the movements of stock prices, there isn't one theory that covers it all.

There is no shortcut for learning the ropes of determining stock prices. This is something that comes along with time and plenty of studying. The more often you engage and practice, the better you will get. It's highly recommended to keep a journal and trade with "fake money" to begin with. This will help you develop your very own strategy. Now that we've covered the basics of what stocks are, along with the principles at play in the market, you are probably wondering how to actually start purchasing stocks.

The Two Main Methods for Buying Stocks:

- **Utilizing Brokerages:** This is probably the most popular way to purchase stocks, and there are two different types of brokerages to be aware of. Using a Full-service brokerage will allow you access to advice from experts who are responsible for managing your investment account. The downside of this is that this method is typically expensive.

- **Using a Discount Brokerage:** These types of brokerages will offer less attention to you personally, leaving you to do most of the work with your investing. However, they have the advantage of costing much less.

There was a time when only rich folks could hire brokers. This is because the full-service brokerages were the only ones available and, as we said, quite expensive. Then the online era came and discount brokers became available over the internet. Now that this is the norm, almost anyone can start investing.

Plans for Direct Investment (DIPs) and Dividend Reinvestment (DRIPs):

DIPs and DRIPs: These are plans used by particular companies, with low fees, that let investors buy stock straight from the business. These are a fantastic way to invest low amounts on a regular basis.

CHAPTER 4: BULLS, BEARS, AND PIGS

If you are a complete beginner, it's possible that you haven't heard about the bears and bulls on Wall Street, but these are some of the most popular and important terms to know.

The Bull Market:

When the market is "bull", the economy is in good shape, stocks are going up in value, people are getting employed, and GDP (gross domestic product) is going up. This makes choosing stocks easier, since they are all rising. However, these conditions can't continue for too long, and can lead to negative scenarios if the overvaluation of stocks occurs. If an investor has optimistic views about a stock, thinking that it will rise, they are referred to as a bull.

The Bear Market:

This type of market has negative conditions, with falling prices in stocks, and even a recession possibly on the horizon. These market conditions make it difficult for investors to choose stocks that will be profitable. One possible way to fix this is to make sure you are earning money as stocks are going down, by short selling. You could also wait out these conditions until you think they are nearly over, only purchasing stock if you expect a bullish market to appear. If an investor has a pessimistic attitude, believing that stocks will be decreasing, they will be said to be a bear.

What Other Animal Terms are Used?

- **Pigs:** This refers to investors who will take large risks, hoping to enjoy huge profits in a small amount of time. They tend to purchase based on advice and tips, investing in businesses without doing enough research. They become emotional, greedy, and impatient about their investment choices, and are also attracted to securities with high risk, all without placing importance on knowing what they're getting into. Expert traders appreciate these types of investors, however, since pigs' losses will lead to profit for bears and bulls.

- **Chickens:** These types of investors live in fear of losing. Their worry tends to override the goal of earning profit, leading them to end up choosing securities on the money-market or to completely opt out of markets. Although it is true that you shouldn't be investing in stocks that make you this nervous, avoidance is not the way to make gains.

Deciding what Category you will Fit into:

Countless strategies and styles for investing exist in the world. Although bears and bulls tend to be at odds with each other, both are able to earn profits along with the cycles that happen with stocks. Even someone with a chicken investing style can enjoy success every so often, but it's rare. The only true profile that loses out consistently is an investor with a pig style.

How to Avoid becoming a Pig Investor:

- **Practice Control of Emotions:** The worst thing you can do when hoping to excel at investing, is allow your emotions to take over and cloud your judgment. Working on stress management, even outside of investing, will help you a lot in this area.

- **Record Success and Failure:** Start a journal and keep track of what moves worked for you, and what didn't. Eventually, you will begin to see some trends that will help you learn to make smart choices, nearly every time.

- **Wait until you're Ready:** Don't jump into trading just because you want to. You need to make sure that you are prepared. This will help you cut your losses.

- **Invest only in what you Understand:** Examine the reasons that you feel compelled to invest in a certain company. Is it wishful thinking? Is it hopes of becoming an overnight millionaire? Take the time to only invest in areas you are knowledgeable about.

Remember, at all times, that having a bullish outlook can help you win, having a bearish outlook can help you win, but adopting the piggish mindset means you always lose.

CHAPTER 5: ASSET ALLOCATION AND DIVERSIFICATION INTRODUCTION

You may not know it, especially if you're new to the world of investment but you might already be aware of some foundational methods for investing smartly and soundly. How would you have learned these? From normal experiences in your life that are completely unrelated to stocks or trading.

A Real-Life Example of Diversification and Risk Reduction:

You can look to an example of vendors on the street to understand this concept. They often sell two unrelated items at their stand, like sunglasses and umbrellas, which doesn't make sense at first glance. These two seemingly opposite items would probably never be purchased at once, but that is the whole idea behind these. On a day when it's raining and people need umbrellas, there will be an upsurge in sales, and the same goes for sunny days with the glasses. When the vendor makes it a point to sell two opposite items, they make sure that they will be earning every day, not just some days. If this example makes sense to you, you are already on your way to having awareness about diversification and the allocation of assets. This chapter will go into depth about both and will also cover how important it is to rebalance your portfolio.

The Basics of Asset Allocation:

The allocation of assets in stocks depends upon dividing your portfolio between multiple categories of assets. For example, these could be bonds, stocks, and cash. Only you can know the appropriate mix of assets to keep in your investment portfolio, since it's a personal choice. Which method will work for you at a certain time is dependent upon how much risk you can take, along with your goals and timeline.

- **Your Trading Time Horizon:** This refers to the amount of months, years, or longer spans of time you plan to invest with the hopes of accomplishing a certain goal, financially. Investors who opt for longer timelines for their goals are more likely to undergo risky investments. They can also partake in volatile environments because they know that they are able to weather the storm of the market. The market natural comes in cycles, ebbing and flowing, and long term investors can take advantage of this.

    On the other hand, some investors are hoping to earn profits for a specific occasion, like college tuition for their kids. In this situation, an investor is less likely to take on risky situations, due to a shorter horizon of time.

- **Your Tolerance for Risk:** This is another important factor to consider, and covers your willingness and ability to lose either all or some of your capital, for the possibility of high returns. Someone who invests aggressively, or has a high tolerance for risk, has a better chance of risking some of their capital for better gains. An investor who is conservative, or has a low tolerance for risk, will likely go for investments that are less risky.

- **Reward vs. Risk:** There is no escaping the fact that reward and risk come together, in the world of investing.

You cannot enjoy success without the possibility of losses. Every single investment you could take comes along with some measure of risk. You have to understand that you could lose all of your money, or part of it, if you have the intention of purchasing any securities (mutual funds, bonds, or stocks).

However, there's a potential reward here, which is the chance at a higher profit. If your goals fit into the long term time line, you will probably earn more due to careful investments in riskier categories (bonds or stocks, for example), instead of only investing in less risky investments. However, only investing in cash could work for goals in the short term.

The Importance of Allocating your Assets:

By being sure to include categories of assets that have moving investment returns, you can protect yourself against devastating risks. You should opt for returns that fluctuate in differing conditions of the market within your investment portfolio. In history, investors' returns from the three main categories of assets haven't performed these movements simultaneously. Conditions of the market that lead to one category performing well will oftentimes lead to another category plummeting, leading to poor returns.

When you invest in multiple categories of assets, you are reducing your overall risk of losing capital. This will also ensure that the returns on investments, overall, will have an easier time in your portfolio. You can rest assuredly knowing that when one category isn't doing well, you have the option to counteract these negative conditions, using a category of assets that have better returns.

Diversification- One of the Most Important Rules of Investing:

Diversification is a method used to spread your capital throughout various investments in order to lower your overall risk. By choosing the correct mix of investments, it's perfectly possible that you could limit the dangers, reduce risk, and remove fluctuations in returns, all without giving up gain potentials. The allocation of assets is of utmost importance, since it plays a major role on the likelihood of you reaching your goals financially. Without including a fair amount of risk on your investment portfolio, you will not likely make enough money to reach your timeline goals.

If you have hopes to meet a goal for the long term, like college or retirement, many experts in finance will tell you to include either mutual funds or basic stocks in your plan. But if you put too many risky choices in your investment portfolio, you may not have access to cash when you find yourself needing it. So if your portfolio is weighed down with mutual funds or stocks, it works for shorter-term goals, like saving for an upcoming trip.

How should you Begin?

Deciding upon the right allocation of your assets is by no means an easy task for an investor. You are essentially attempting to choose a combination of assets that has the best chance to meet your personal goals, with a risk level that is tolerable to your circumstances. Once you are close to reaching your financial goals, you have to mix them up again, adjusting accordingly with your new circumstances. Here are some options you can look into for your asset allocation:

- **Creating a Model Yourself:** If you have a clear understanding of risk tolerance and goal timelines, and also have a bit of experience in investing, you might feel alright with making up your own model for asset allocation. There are plenty of general rules, along with investing books and online sources that will help in your research and choices.

- **Consulting a Professional:** Many experts in finance believe that deciding upon the allocation of your assets is the most serious of all choices you can make in terms of investing. Some even say that it has more importance than the investments you decide to purchase. Holding this in mind, it might be worth considering professional advice. This could aid you in determining the allocation you will begin with and also possibly adjustments you can make down the road. Before you decide to consult a professional, however, do your homework on their credentials and success history with investing.

Whether you opt for professional guidance or not, research is important. Some online sources provide a calculator for helping you determine how you should allocate assets. Sources aside, however, this is your own choice, and there is no magical model for asset allocation that works for every person or every goal. You have to opt for what works for your life and money goals.

How are Diversification and Asset Allocation Related?

We've all heard the age old wisdom against placing all of your eggs into a single basket. Diversification can be seen as following this advice. The method here involves investing across different avenues in hopes that when one doesn't do so well, your other investment choices will earn enough to cover what you lost. A lot of investors utilize the allocation of assets for diversifying investments throughout categories of assets, while other people who invest choose not to.

Investing almost completely in stocks, for example, for someone in their twenties starting a retirement fun, could work under specific circumstances. A family hoping to save up for a house investing completely in cash equivalents could also work under very specific circumstances. But neither circumstance is doing much to lessen risk by looking to other categories of assets. So selecting a model for allocation of assets will not automatically make your portfolio more diverse. What determines how diverse your investment portfolio is, is the way you spread out your capital among various investment types.

How to Know if you're Properly Diversified:

A portfolio that has been properly diversified should be so in two main respects; within the categories of assets, and between the categories of assets.

- **Within and Between Categories:** This means that you should allocate investments between cash equivalents, bonds, and stocks, along with any other categories of assets, but also spread the investments out inside of each category. The trick to doing this right is making sure that you decide on investments in parts of each category that could perform in various ways under various conditions of the market.

- **Identify Companies and Invest Accordingly:** One sure way you can diversify the investments in your portfolio within a particular category, is to find and choose to invest in a variety of industry sectors and businesses.

- **At Least 12 Stocks:** You won't be properly diversified if you are only investing in five stocks individually. You have to have a minimum of 12 stocks, carefully selected, to enjoy true diversification and optimal risk protection.

Using Mutual Funds for Diversification:

Since truly accomplishing a diversified portfolio can be difficult, some people choose to do so within each of their categories, by owning mutual funds, instead of going through investments from each category of assets. Mutual funds are businesses that gather money from multiple investors, putting that money toward financial instruments, along with bonds and stocks. These types of funds make it easier for investors to have ownership of small parts of multiple investments. Index funds in the stock market, for example, already own shares in hundreds (or even thousands) of different businesses. Since it's only one investment to you, this is a great choice for diversifying.

Keep in mind, though, that mutual funds do not always equal diversification instantly, particularly when a fund is mainly focused on a specific sector of industry. Investing in mutual funds that have a narrow focus will mean that you're more likely to have to invest in multiple funds to get adequate diversification in your portfolio. We will go into greater detail about mutual funds in a later chapter of the book.

- **Diversifying Within Categories:** When it comes to working within categories of assets, this could translate to considering large stock funds, along with international and smaller business stock funds.

- **Diversifying Between Categories:** In this situation, it could mean thinking about money market, bond, and stock funds. Don't forget to consider fees, since you will probably pay extra for this, which takes away from your overall potential gains. Always take costs and fees into consideration when it comes to diversification of your investment portfolio.

<u>Switching up the Allocation of your Assets:</u>

The main reason why people end up changing their allocation is changes to the timelines of their financial goals. To say it another way, as you find yourself getting closer to goals of your investment, you will probably have to change allocation of your assets. The majority of people, for example, who invest in their retirement will be holding less stock and a higher amount of cash equivalents and bonds as they near the age of retirement. You might also have to change up the allocation of your assets if your goal, money situation, or tolerance of risk undergoes any changes.

But experts at investing do not usually switch up their allocation due to performance on a relative scale of categories. This could mean increasing the amount of stocks they hold in their portfolio when the market is active and hot. Rather, they take these opportunities to look at their portfolios and rebalance them. The topic of rebalancing will be discussed in detail in the last chapter of this book.

CHAPTER 6: POPULAR INVESTMENT CLASSES

There is something out there in the world of investment for everyone. Stocks, mutual funds, bonds, funds for your lifestyle, exchange traded funds, and more. However, in this chapter, we will start with the three main categories of assets.

Asset Categories to be Familiar with:

- **Stocks:** Out of the three main categories of assets, stocks are known to have the best returns and also the highest risks. When considered as an asset, stocks are the hardest hitting aspect of a portfolio, offering the best potential chance for financial growth and success. This means that they win big, but also lose.

  How volatile stocks are means that they are highly risky in terms of shorter financial goals. Business stocks on a large, group scale have suffered losses about a third of the time, and at times these have been quite extensive. However, investors who have been able to stick out the volatility of stocks within longer time periods have been able to enjoy quality returns.

- **Cash Equivalents and Cash:** This section refers to treasury bills, certificates of deposit, savings deposits, money market funds, and more. They are known as the safest of all possible investments, meaning that they give back the least out of the three main categories of assets. The risk of losing any of your capital in this category is very, very low.

Multiple investments are guaranteed by the federal government using cash or cash equivalents. Losses in investments in equivalents that are not guaranteed can happen at times, but very rarely. The main worry that investors choosing this category will undergo is the risk of inflation. The risk here is that inflation could happen at a faster rate than returns and end up eating into the money in the account.

- **Bonds:** These are, on average, lower volatility than stocks, meaning that their returns will be more modest. The result here is that investors getting close to their goals financially may increase their bond holdings, in relation to their stock holdings, due to the lowered risk. The lowered risk of having more bonds in their portfolio would be an attractive prospect, even though they have a lower growth potential than stocks. Remember that specific groups of bonds do offer returns that are high enough to rival stocks, but these types (called junk bonds or high yield bonds) come with a higher level of risk.

Stocks, cash equivalents, and bonds are the best-known of all categories of assets, and what you would be choosing between when looking to start a fund for college or retirement. However, there are other categories, such as precious metals, real estate, and more, that are out there. Some investors may want to include these categories as well for even more diversification. These categories usually come along with their own unique risks, so before deciding to invest, make sure you are aware of these and that they align with your plans.

More about Mutual Funds:

We already discussed them a bit earlier in the book, but a mutual fund is a grouping of bonds, stocks, or various other asset types. This grouping of assets is managed by a financial company, since the investor doesn't have the necessary knowledge, resources, or time to purchase securities that are diversified by themselves. In exchange for this service, investors will be charged a fee by the fund, which could be about 1 percent annually. When it comes to the majority of stock funds, a portfolio manager selects the holdings, deciding on stocks that they believe to perform the best, and avoiding the ones that don't show promise. This method is known as actively managing the account, but there are other methods for running mutual funds.

An Overview of Index Funds:

Index funds follow a different method than mutual funds. Rather than choosing only stocks which are expected to perform well, the index fund will purchase all share within a specific index. The goal here is the replication of the whole market's performance. But since these types of funds purchase and hold instead of frequently trading, and don't call for or require any research of businesses, they cost a lot less to run.

Why Average Works best for Long Term Investing:

At first glance, this method may seem counter-intuitive. Why would you want to purchase all of the stocks within a particular market, only to earn average stock returns? Because research has proven that active managing comes with such higher fees, along with the difficulty of choosing stocks that will win, leading to losses overall. Active funds, though they sound great on the service, haven't been able to deliver quality performance, overall.

A General Overview of ETFs:

So based on the information we just gave, index funds sound like the smarter choice, but which type is the best to opt for? There are two main types to know about; the traditional options, or the exchange-traded options. You will get comparable results from each, but they have differing structures. To begin with, a mutual fund will enable you to purchase and sell stocks in a direct way with the company related to the funds. That company will allow you to trade once per day, in relation to the closing price of that day.

Why Traditional Index Funds might be Preferred by Some:

But ETFs are not directly sold by the companies of these funds. Rather, you need to have an account for brokerage, for purchasing and selling these shares, and they are displayed on the exchange. This sounds convenient and ideal, but you pay for this convenience. Similar to stocks, a commission must be paid by investors to the brokerage each time they sell or purchase.

This means that investors who use smaller amounts will find the more traditional methods more affordable. If you get stuck with a lot of costs for trading, it ends up taking away a lot from your returns. However, since these funds are exchange traded, the shares are available for trading during the entire day. The ability to trade throughout a day is a popular and well-liked perk for a lot of investors. The last 10 years have proven that ETFs are growing quickly compared to other options.

CHAPTER 7: MANAGING YOUR INVESTMENT PORTFOLIO

Is it possible to only put a few hours of work in per year, and still beat out most investors? Yes it is, with index funds and smart choices. Learning how to be a "boring" or "plan vanilla" investor, is actually the smartest strategy of all, and will ensure that you don't have to be glued to your computer to profit. Not letting yourself succumb to new swings in the market will help you stay on track and focus more on small details that can add up to great returns in the long run.

The Benefits of Opting for an Index Fund:

These types of funds are beneficial for many reasons, but mainly the ratios of low expense and the diversification that comes along with them. When you buy an index fund's shares, you automatically gain access to a whole index. This balances out the appreciation and depreciation of stocks, lowering risk.

Habits to Get into for Success in the Stock Market with Minimal Hours:

It's possible to fare better than 80 percent of investors, with the right knowledge and attitude. We all have dreams to earn big and enjoy the freedom that comes along with it, so here are some moves to make for a millionaire mindset.

- **Learn to Embrace Passivity:** This may sound counter-intuitive, since success is usually stereotypically about aggressively chasing your goals, but it's true, passivity will help you with investing.

- **Get in the Know:** All people who are considerably wealthy investors know that index funds which are passively managed, along with ETFs, outperform funds that are actively managed when it comes to the long term, since they have lower fees.

Remember to Diversify:

We have mentioned this a few times in the book, due to how important it is. But among the many great reasons to diversify, there is one that stands out most. The market that existed in '82 does not exist anymore. The one that comes next will be controlled by entirely different factors. While the previous market was driven by spending from the last generation (the Baby Boomers), this generation is now entering retirement, which means lower spending. This, in addition to the amount of private debt that stretches across all ages, makes diversification of the utmost importance. Economies aren't able to grow sustainably when huge debts are in the picture. Does this mean that index funds aren't a good idea? Absolutely not, they simply need to be used as tools for investing for the long term. They are much safer than individual level stocks.

Why do Mutual Funds Fail?

It's true, mutual funds fail sometimes. This is mainly because, unlike accounts with established banks, no insurance agency exists to protect investors against rough patches or complete failure. Here are some other examples of hazards for failure of mutual funds.

- **A Negative Cycle:** One of the most common situations here is a fund making the wrong choice at a bad time, creating a cycle that spins out of control and brings the fund down with it. This happens when people go all-in on certain stocks when they start to show promise, leading the bubble to pop and holdings to start heading to the red. Investors will then see this happening, along with their shares depreciating each day. Soon, sellers will multiply, creating a cycle of pressure that brings the fund, as a whole, down.

- **No Guarantees:** This was mentioned in an earlier chapter, and it applies here as well. When it comes to investing in stocks, there is simply no way to guarantee that thing will work out, unless your broker can offer some type of product (usually a hybrid) with a safety net that has been clearly outlined. Typically, these types of hybrid products come along with expensive costs, so make sure you do your homework before committing. This is true even with funds being offered by your trusted banker.

You may believe that since the mutual fund has the name of a bank on it and gets offered right next to CDs (certificates of deposit) and savings accounts, it has more protection than other investments. But the truth is, this fund is unprotected at the same level of other stocks. Here is some more information to know about mutual funds.

Fees- A Big Issue with Mutual Funds:

Fees are, arguably, the largest issue that exists when it comes to mutual funds. These fees will end up playing a toll on your overall return, and are responsibly for many funds performing in a subpar manner. Worse than this is the methods mutual fund industries will use to hide these fees, using jargon and financial complications. Many experts claim that companies in the mutual fund industry can get away with charging these fees, because the average person investing has a hard time understanding exactly where their money is going.

The Two Main Types of Fees to be Aware of:

There are two main fee types you will encounter with mutual funds, so keep an eye out for both of them.

- Fees for transaction when you sell or buy shares within a mutual fund.

- Costs on a yearly basis that are intended to keep you invested.

Your Mutual Fund or Financial Manager might be Getting Richer than you:

In some cases, financial advisers and managers of mutual funds end up making even more than you do off of the money you invest. But let's cover some important details first. There are countless organizations and people in the industry of finance who have the responsibility of investing the money of others. This will include hedge funds and mutual funds, and also wealth and asset managers. These two sections overlap a lot of the time and are told apart by the person regulating them and the guidelines they must adhere to. To make this more complicated, wealth managers can also be referred to as financial advisers. This is because they help people with planning of finances and investing. For the remainder of this section, we will call them wealth managers.

What do Wealth Managers share in Common with Each other?

One overlapping quality in these particular managers is the method they are compensated by. Most of them charge a fee for management, which is a specific percentage of the entire sum of the money they are managing. This fee gets taken out of your fund and placed into the pocket of the manager each year. When this is just a year you're thinking about, this isn't hard to comprehend, and doesn't sound too unreasonable either.

Annual Fees start to Add up over the Years:

However, when you choose the same manager to hold onto your funds every year, these costs start to add up over time, which some investors have a hard time understanding fully. Each year, this cost gets charged, meaning that a little more is taken from your overall worth, each and every year, regardless of the state of your investments. Whether your money is shrinking or growing, the same percentage gets deducted from your net worth. These slices end up adding up to quite a sizeable amount.

Maximizing Savings for Taxes using an IRA or 401K:

401K accounts are funded using dollars that are "pre-taxed", meaning that whatever you contribute gets deducted from paychecks previous to taxes being deducted. In other words, if you're funding your 401K, the income amount you're paying taxes for is being lowered. This can end up softening the hit your pay takes.

This means that if you're making small additions to your account, or increasing these additions by about 1 percent yearly, you will likely not even notice what is missing from your paychecks. The bill for your taxes will end up being lower. Of course, you will need to pay your taxes at some point, but you can worry about this once you reach the age of retirement. You will get taxed by the IRS at the typical tax rate of your income bracket.

How should you Re-balance?

Once you have come up with a strategy for allocating assets that fits with your lifestyle and financial goals, you may find that factors have changed within your portfolio and its asset classes. How does this occur? Throughout a year, every security in the portfolio has experienced a change in the market value, and led to a return of a different amount. This leads to change in weighting of your assets. Rebalancing your portfolio is similar to doing basic car maintenance. It will let investors maintain their level of risk, minimizing possible dangers.

When to take Action with Rebalancing:

There are two main ways that people choose to identify when they need to rebalance.

- **A Specified Time Schedule:** Your rebalancing can be done passed on a time schedule, which is recommended by countless experts in finance. Every half year to full year should be sufficient. The benefit here is that you will be reminded regularly to perform this necessary function.

- **As Needed:** Rather than relying on the calendar, you can rely on your own judgment as to when it's necessary to rebalance. Some say that you should rebalance the portfolio only when asset weights have gone off balance to what you previously decided upon. The beneficial aspect of this way is that you will be told by your investments when this is needed.

Whichever method you choose, remember that this act is most effective when performed infrequently. Twice a year is the maximum frequency you should do this with.

What does Rebalancing your Portfolio really Entail?

The process of rebalancing involves selling and purchasing segments of your investment portfolio, with the goal of setting each class of assets back to their original positions. Also, if the risk tolerance or strategy for investment has changed for an investor, they can rebalance in order to readjust each asset class or security's weightings. This will help to fulfill the allocation of assets that have been devised in a new and more appropriate way for their situation.

Does Past Performance indicate Future Performance?

Many investors think that if one of their investments enjoyed success during the past 12 months, it should do the same for the following year. However, the way an investment performed over the last year does not always indicate how it will move in the future. This is something that mutual funds are careful to disclose, most of the time. A lot of investors, though, stay invested heavily in the fun on account of the wins of last year, and might end up investing more heavily in that fund, even if it is losing. Keep in mind that equities tend to have more volatility than securities with fixed incomes, meaning that the gains of last year could turn into losses in the year ahead.

Keeping your Portfolio in Alignment with Financial Goals:

Investors rebalance to make sure their portfolios remain comparable to the initial mix of asset allocation. This act is needed because investments don't always stay on track with your financial goals on their own. Some of them may grow quicker than other investments. When you rebalance, you make sure your investment portfolio is not overshooting on any categories of assets, returning the portfolio to the appropriate risk level for you.

This could mean that you started out deciding that stocks will take up 70 percent of the investment portfolio, then come to see that the market increased and they now represent 90 percent. This will require you selling off a few of your investments in stocks or buying investments from a category that is under-represented, to stay true to your initial allocation of assets combination. When an investor goes to rebalance their portfolio, they must review each category. If any investment does not align with their goals, they have to adjust accordingly to keep things in balance.

Three Differing Methods for Rebalancing:

There are a few different methods you can choose when you decide that rebalancing your portfolio is necessary.

- **Make some Sales:** The first option is to sell some investments from a category that has too much weight, using the earnings to buy assets in categories that are under-weight.

- **Purchase**: You can also make the choice of buying new investments for categories that are under-weight.

- **Regular Contributions**: If you already have a habit of contributing regularly to your investment portfolio, you can adjust these additions so that under-weight categories come back into harmony with the rest of the categories.

Consider this, before Rebalancing:

Before taking steps to rebalance, you need to think about whether your chosen method will bring about new consequences for taxes or higher fees for transactions. Contact a professional advisor to aid you in identifying methods for minimizing possible fees or tax additions.

- **Stay Committed to Financial Goals:** It may be tough to shift money from a category that is doing great, but it's a necessary action and keeps you on track with your financial goals. Decide ahead of time that you will do this, so that you stick with it.

- **Purchase Low, Sell High:** When you take away from the investments that are winning currently, to help out investments that are losing, you will have no choice but to purchase low and sell high. This is a great strategy for investment.

How to Find out More about your Tolerance for Risk:

There are plenty of free resources out there that will allow you to find out more about your own risk tolerance.

- **Questionnaires Online:** Look up free questionnaires given out by mutual fund businesses, publications for investment, and other various financial sources. On some websites, you will receive guidance on allocating assets based on your answers.

    Although these suggestions are helpful, especially to beginners, remember that you could be viewing biased results geared toward convincing individuals to purchase related products.

- **Analysis Tools:** As soon as you've begun investing, you will be given access to resources on the internet that will help you with portfolio management. For example, mutual fund business webpages offer customers a tool for analyzing their portfolio. Looking at the results from these tests can aid you in allocating your assets appropriately. They will also help you find out if you're properly diversified or need rebalancing.

Take advantage of free tools, but remember that there is no substitute for plenty of practice, when it comes to investing.

CONCLUSION

Thank you again for downloading this book!

I hope this book was able to help you to see the importance of starting to save as early as you can, and provide you with some valuable tips you can apply to your life to begin your investment journey. The sooner you start to plan for your future, the better off you will be. Life is full of unforeseen circumstances, so get ahead of them now by starting while you're still young, instead of missing out on great opportunities to grow your wealth.

The next step is to take what you have learned and begin applying it immediately. Once you have a decent savings account, there is no reason that you cannot grow your income and secure your future. Living paycheck to paycheck means that you are not protected in case some type of emergency comes up, so plan ahead while you still can!

Finally, if you enjoyed this book, then I'd like to ask you for a favor, would you be kind enough to leave a review for this book on Amazon? It'd be greatly appreciated! Thank you and good luck!

www.ingramcontent.com/pod-product-compliance
Lightning Source LLC
Chambersburg PA
CBHW070335190526
45169CB00005B/1899